NATIONAL
GEOGRAPHIC
KiDS

CAT SCIENCE UNLEASHED

FUN ACTIVITIES TO DO WITH YOUR FELINE FRIEND

JODI WHEELER-TOPPEN

PHOTOGRAPHS BY
MATTHEW RAKOLA

NATIONAL GEOGRAPHIC
WASHINGTON, D. C.

CONTENTS

FIT FELINES

SENSATIONAL SENSES

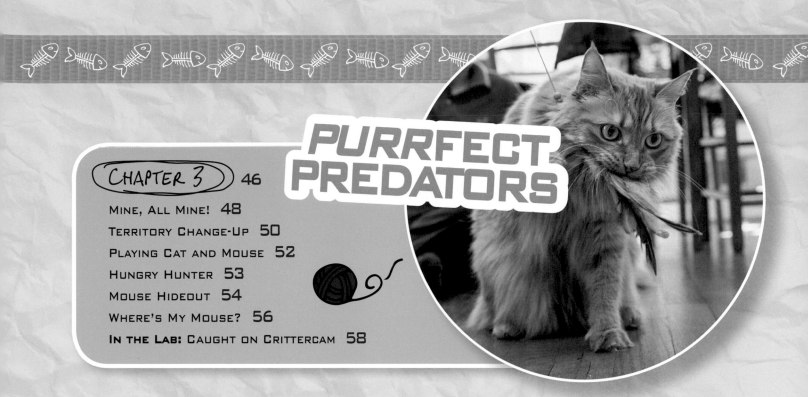

PURRFECT PREDATORS

CLEVER KITTIES

INTRODUCTION

Is there anything as *purr*fect as a fluffy feline flopped in your lap? Or as cute as a kitty curled up for a catnap? Or as prone to catastrophe as a kitten practicing his pouncing? It's no wonder that cats are one of the most common pets in the world. Even so, these feline friends remain something of a mystery to humans.

How do cats hunt, purr, or squeeze into tight spaces? What are their favorite smells, flavors, and sounds? Why are they so dainty as they drink and so lucky as they fall? And just what goes on in their mysterious minds?

Get ready to find out! You'll discover tons of fantastic feline science on every page of this book. Complete the hands-on activities to explore the science behind your cat's senses, how your kitty is built to move, how your cat sees the world, and so much more.

Some of the activities in this book dig into science that will be the same for all cats, whether they are solemn snugglers or feisty fur balls. Other activities are designed to help you understand the most important kitty on Earth: your own. And, believe it or not, your little puffball actually wants to do science with you: The activities in this book will get your cat's body and brain moving, and she'll be healthier and happier because of it.

So pounce on this chance to do science with the sweetest, softest, and most mischievous lab partner you'll ever find— your cat!

 SAFETY GUIDELINES AND TIPS

Dear Parents,

Each page in this book has been designed to actively engage your child in fun, creative, and challenging ways. While we recommend that your young scientist have adult supervision for ALL of the projects in this book, certain activities REQUIRE adult supervision and SHOULD NOT be conducted UNLESS an ADULT is actively involved. We have flagged those activities with red labels that say "Grab a Grown-Up."

Before you begin an activity, please read and discuss the following SAFETY GUIDELINES with your child:

- Be careful during the activities, and only an adult should work with tools such as sharp knives or scissors.

- Even a cat that you know well can scratch or bite unexpectedly. Watch for signs your cat is unhappy, and avoid touching areas where your cat is sensitive (e.g., many cats do not like to be touched along their bellies).

- Prepare yourself to work in a safe manner (e.g., wear long sleeves if your cat is prone to scratching). Create a safe work space (e.g., a fenced-in yard).

- Use safety equipment (e.g., have a first aid kit in the house).

- Wash and dry your hands before and after each activity.

- Follow the directions for each activity and take your time.

- Read and follow the safety tips on applicable activities and the guidelines on all product labels, and use your own common sense and judgment.

CAT SAFETY

The activities in this book are designed to be fun for both kids and their pets. Just like humans, cats enjoy new challenges! Please review these guidelines with your child to make sure any participating kitty is safe, comfortable, and having fun.

- Only do these activities with a cat that knows your child well and is comfortable around your child.

- Watch for signs that the cat is unhappy. If any of these activities seem to make the cat uncomfortable or upset, stop immediately.

- Even a cat that is enjoying an activity needs a break. Make sure the cat has access to water throughout these activities and if he wants to stop, let him.

- If your cat is on a special diet, check with his veterinarian before feeding him treats. Always check with the cat's owner before you feed him anything.

- Clean up when you are done, so your kitty doesn't accidentally eat any leftover materials.

- If you decide to alter an activity or try a new version, make sure the new plan is safe for both your child and the cat.

HOW TO USE THIS BOOK

Science experiments are often worked out through trial and error, and cats can be unpredictable. Because cats come in so many shapes, sizes, and personalities, not every activity will work with every kitty. Some experiments may work better than others, and others may not work at all. Don't be discouraged—you're in good company! Even the cat scientists interviewed in this book had challenges making their experiments work. Alexis Noel (p. 44) made several models of cat tongues before she came up with a successful one. And Kristyn Vitale (p. 74) designed her entire study—finding out what motivates cats—because the cats she was using in a different project were not cooperating!

Let your cat in on the exploration. He'll be happier if you give him a chance to study, sniff, and rub each object you will use in an activity. If your cat isn't eager to try something the way it is described, find a method he likes better. For example, if he seems skittish of the feather apparatus used in "Awesome Odors" (p. 42), try putting the odors on cotton balls scattered across the floor. Or simply walk away and pretend you aren't paying attention. Some of the cats who tested the activities for this book became braver if they thought no one was looking. You might also consider time of day. "Tracking Tabby" (p. 24) and "Hungry Hunter" (p. 53) will help you find the times of day when your cat is naturally more active.

On the other hand, if you find an activity that your cat seems to enjoy, stay with it! Some activities give suggestions for going further, but you can always brainstorm new ideas to expand on any of the experiments. The possibilities are endless. Just remember to give your cat a break when he seems to be tired of playing, and reward him with positive reinforcement, such as tasty treats, behind-the-ear scratches, and encouraging words!

RIGHTY OR LEFTY

WHICH PAW DOES YOUR CAT PREFER?

Difficulty Level:
Medium

Active Time Needed:
45 minutes

It's not just people who favor one hand over the other. Your cat probably uses one paw more easily as well. Since you can't just hand her a pen to see how she writes, play these games to find her preferred paw.

YOU NEED

jelly jar treat trap (see p. 71)
butter or tuna treat
toy on a string
painter's tape
pencil and paper

TIP
Make sure you place the jar and the toy directly in front of your cat, so she won't just use the paw closest to the object.

2

TAKE IT FURTHER
To get strong results, scientists generally test paw preference many times over several days. One recent study tested each cat 100 times over 10 days on three different tasks. To be certain of your cat's paw preference, keep collecting data on these tasks over several days.

Some of these experiments were just begging for more exploration. Some of our ideas and questions are listed. You can come up with more!

Before you start, check the difficulty and time required. Some activities need a helping hand from an adult.

Pay attention to special safety notes that will help you—and your cat—have the best experience.

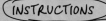

4

INSTRUCTIONS

1 Gather your materials for all three tests. You need to repeat each experiment 10 times. For best results, switch between the activities until you have completed 10 trials of all three so your cat doesn't get bored.

2 For the first test, place the toy on a string in front of your cat. Slowly pull it away from her in a straight line. Record the first paw she uses to swipe at the toy. If she grabs with both paws at the same time, try the test again.

3 For the second test, place butter or tuna in the bottom of the jar. Set it in front of your cat. Record the first paw your cat uses to reach for the treat.

4 For the third test, place a bit of painter's tape on the bridge of your cat's nose. Record the first paw she uses to try to remove it.

5 Add the number of times your cat used her left and right paw. If she used one paw at least 20 times across all of the experiments, then your cat favors that paw.

⚠️ SAFETY NOTE
Be sure you only use painter's tape in this activity so that you don't damage her sensitive fur or skin.

THE RIGHT FOOT
Does your cat have a paw preference? Experiments indicate that most cats—90 percent or more—use one paw more often than the other. They seem to be divided about equally between righties and lefties, although males may be left-pawed more often than females. Cats are more likely to use their dominant hand when doing a complicated task. This is similar to a human—you might grab a book off the table with whatever hand is, well, handy. But you are going to be pickier about the hand you use with a screwdriver. Getting the treat out of the jar or wiping off her nose are complicated tasks for a cat, so she may have used the same paw for almost every try. Grabbing for a toy is less challenging, so cats are less likely to show a dominant paw for that task.

Each chapter has fun creations you can make that will enrich your cat's life, even after the research is done!

Even a simple activity can have tricky bits. Our young scientists and their kitties helped find the finicky spots and ways to make things go more smoothly.

MEET OUR SCIENTISTS AND CATS

SAMUEL, 11 & HONEY, 7

TEAGAN, 10

PIPPA, 1 YEAR
(CAMERA SHY)

DUNCAN, 7 MONTHS,
BASIL, 1 YEAR, DIGBY, 6 MONTHS

ENZO, 12 & OZZY, 9

DAXXON, 10
& NICHOLAS, 3

ERIN, 14 & ARWEN, 3

Oxford, 12 & Bob, 15

Tovi, 11 & Bob, 15

Miles, 7 & Truman, 8

Harrison, 14 & Elsa, 7

Daniela, 12 & Ashton, 6

Grant, 12 & Truman, 8

CHAPTER 1

FIT FELINES

THE BASICS OF YOUR CAT'S FORM

Cats sometimes seem to defy the very laws of physics. They balance like elite gymnasts on curtain rods, leap gracefully to the top of tall cabinets, curl up in bowls, and always seem to land on their feet. Cats slink, scurry, scamper, and, of course, snooze. How on Earth do they coordinate all those moves?

Beneath their fluffy coats, cats have a skeleton and muscles, just like you do. Those muscles pull the bones to create movement. And like yours, a cat's heart and lungs provide oxygen to keep things going. But cats also have special **adaptations** that allow them to pull off maneuvers that you might find tricky, like squishing into tight spaces, balancing on thin ledges, and drinking using only their tongues.

Get ready to learn more about the science of cats in action.

TERRIFIC TOUCHDOWNS

I f you've ever seen your cat slip from the back of the couch, you'll know that cats are experts at falling. Like fancy gymnasts, they twist, turn, and—voilà!—land triumphantly on all fours. How do kitties land on their feet even when they start falling upside down? It doesn't seem like it should be possible to turn over midair with nothing to push against. It might look like magic, but the maneuver is actually a series of movements made possible by a cat's unique body. Scientists call this the cat righting **reflex.**

TUCK AND ROLL

At the beginning of the fall, your kitty tucks his front legs and extends his back legs. This lets his front half spin faster than his haunches, just as an ice skater spins faster when her arms are by her side and slower when she holds them out.

Famous artist Leonardo da Vinci sketched cats in different positions because he was fascinated by their flexibility.

BACK END BEND

The cat sticks out his front legs to slow the rotation of his front half and draws his back legs under him to allow the back of his body to flip over.

KEEPING KITTY SAFE

Despite their amazing righting reflex, cats can still get hurt in a fall. Cats who fall out of the window of a high-rise may break a leg. And cats who fall short distances may not have time to twist around. You can protect your cat from falls by keeping screens in your windows and watching him closely if you take him onto a balcony. Still, when you see a cat on the roof, it's good to know that he'll probably get himself down safely.

AN EAR FOR BALANCE

To pull off a foot-first landing, your cat has to know how his body is moving relative to the ground. The most important tool for flipping and balancing is found deep inside those pointy ears. Of course, a cat's ears hold the bones and membranes needed for hearing, but they also contain an apparatus to help the cat feel his head movements. It's called the **vestibular organ,** and it is made of three round tubes that stick out in three different directions. The tubes contain hairs that connect to nerve cells and are full of fluid. When a cat moves, turns his head, or changes speed, the fluid sloshes around and shakes the hairs. The hairs trigger the nerve cells to send a quick message to the brain, which can kick-start the balancing act if needed.

HANG LOOSE

Loose connections between the bones in his back allow a cat to turn the front and back of his body separately.

Cat claws curve toward their paws, like tiny hooks. This works fabulously for climbing up a tree, but to climb down, a cat has to go backward.

TOUCH DOWN

His legs work like springs to soften the landing.

⚠ SAFETY NOTE
Never drop a cat to test his righting reflexes.
He would not enjoy the experience,
and it is possible for him to be hurt in a fall.

FELINE FINE

TAKE YOUR CAT'S VITAL SIGNS

> **Difficulty Level:**
> **Medium**

> **Active Time Needed:**
> **15 minutes**

You take your cat to the vet. After you survive getting her into her carrier, listening to the howling in the car, and dodging the looks that suggest she wants to eat you alive, you finally get to the exam room. And the first thing the veterinarian does? Take Kitty's vital signs. Your vet knows that a steady heartbeat and regular breathing will keep your kitty on the go. You can try taking her vital signs right in your house—no howling required.

YOU NEED

timer or watch with second hand
stethoscope

TAKE A DEEP BREATH

With each breath, Fluffy's lungs fill with air and let it go. The main muscle responsible for breathing stretches across the bottom of the rib cage, and is called the **diaphragm.** When the diaphragm tightens, it opens up her lungs so air can rush in. As long as your cat is relaxed and comfortable, she'll take between 16 and 40 breaths per minute. That's probably similar to your own **respiration** rate. Next time she's sprawled out on the floor enjoying some sunshine, lie next to her, match her breathing, and catch a catnap of your own.

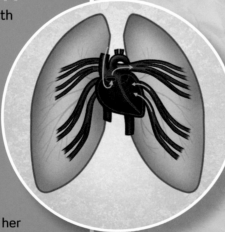

INSTRUCTIONS

RESPIRATION RATE:

1 While your cat is relaxing, watch her chest to see her ribs rise and fall.

2 Count the number of times her ribs rise over the course of 15 seconds. If you have difficulty seeing the breaths, try softly laying your hand on her side to feel them.

3 Multiply that number by four to get the number of breaths in a minute. This is your cat's resting respiration rate.

1

TIP
It will be easiest to hear a heartbeat if you work in a quiet place.

SAFETY NOTE
If your cat seems irritated by the stethoscope, stop. She may be more willing to let you listen at another time.

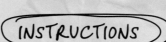

INSTRUCTIONS

HEART RATE:

1 While your cat is calmly sitting or lying down, gently rest the end of your stethoscope against the left side of your cat's chest, just behind her elbow. You may need to place a hand on her other side to stabilize her as you listen.

2 Listen for a heartbeat. If you don't hear it right away, slowly and gently shift your stethoscope around until you find it.

3 Count the number of beats that you hear over the course of 15 seconds.

4 Multiply the number of beats you counted by four. This will tell you how many times her heart beats in one minute.

MATTERS OF THE HEART

When Kitty goes for a flying leap, her muscles need a steady supply of oxygen. They'll get that oxygen from the blood, and it's her heart that keeps the blood flowing. The heart is a two-sided pump. The right side sends blood on a short trip to her lungs to pick up oxygen. The blood zips back to the left side of the heart, where a forceful squeeze sends it all over Kitty's body. The left side of the heart is stronger, and it sends blood the farthest. If it sounds like her heart is racing, that's because it is. The average resting heart rate for a cat is between 120 and 200 beats per minute. That's about two to three times faster than yours.

BALANCING ACT

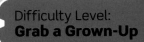

DISCOVER HOW A CAT STAYS STABLE

> Difficulty Level:
> **Grab a Grown-Up**

> Active Time Needed:
> **10 minutes**

If you've ever walked across a balance beam, you know how much concentration it takes to keep your balance. But cats make it seem easy. Tiptoeing across a tiny handrail? No problem. Slinking across a small shelf? *Pfft*—too easy! Coax Kitty to show off his balancing skills while you study the movements that keep him on top.

YOU NEED

2 x 4-foot (0.6 x 1.2-m) wood board
    that is at least 5.5 feet (1.7 m) long
treat or toy
two chairs or other furniture
    of equal height
old towels

INSTRUCTIONS

1 Position your chairs so they face each other and are far enough apart that the board fits between them.

2 Have an adult help you place the board across the chairs to create a balance beam. Push on the board. If it is shaky, arrange the towels under the board so that it wiggles as little as possible.

3 Allow your cat to sniff and explore the balance beam.

4 Carefully place your cat on one of the chairs. Show him the treat or toy. Slowly move the treat or toy to the middle of the beam, keeping it just out of reach so your cat walks across the balance beam in pursuit of his reward.

5 Notice how your cat moves across the narrow space. How does he hold his tail? How does he move his legs? Where is he looking?

6 When your cat is almost across the board, give him the treat or toy. Observe how he maintains his balance as he enjoys the treat or attacks the toy.

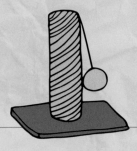

Consider asking an adult to video your cat in action. You can check the video later for movements you may have missed.

SAFETY NOTE
Have an adult help you make sure the board is secure and stable. Do not force your cat to go on the balance beam if he doesn't want to.

6

CROUCHING KITTY

Your cat eases across the board, carefully placing one foot in front of the other, keeping his feet almost in a straight line. If he wobbles, he can fine-tune his body placement more easily than a person, because the **vertebrae** in his spine are connected to each other more loosely. Your cat may crouch as he walks. This lowers his center of gravity, making it less likely that he'll fall over. Some of the time, your cat may hold his tail low and taut directly behind him. But if he needs to shift his body in one direction, he'll swing his tail in the other, to balance out the weight and keep himself firmly on top of the board.

HAPPY HIDEAWAY

BUILD A SECRET FORT FOR YOUR CAT

So you bought your kitty an expensive cat tower, spent hours setting it up, and even threw in some tempting cat toys ... but she only has eyes for the box it came in. What?! Cats love small spaces where they feel enclosed and protected. Build this hideaway and use it with "The Shrinking Cat" on p. 22 to create the ideal escape for those times when your kitty needs some privacy.

1

2

3

4

YOU NEED

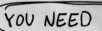

box large enough for your cat
 to stand inside
box cutter
4 paper plates
safety scissors
drawing compass or series of circles
 of different sizes to trace
pencil
paints or markers

INSTRUCTIONS

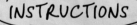

1 Open the compass so that it will draw a circle a little smaller than your paper plates. Use that setting to draw a circle on the side of the large box. If your box is a rectangle, put the circle on one of the smaller sides of the box.

2 Have an adult cut out the circle with the box cutter.

3 On your first paper plate, use the compass to draw a circle that is a little smaller than the hole on your box. Cut the hole out of the paper plate.

4 Repeat with three other plates, making the circle a little smaller each time.

5 Tape the plate with the largest hole to the box. Tape the plate with the next largest hole to the first plate. Repeat until all of the plates are taped, with the smallest hole in front.

6 Decorate the box with your kitty's name and pictures of her favorite things.

7 You will be able to remove the plates one at a time to make the hole bigger until you find the opening that allows your cat to enter the box. Your cat will love having a safe space with an opening so small that only she can get in.

TIP
It may be easier to hold the compass still and have a helper rotate the plates to draw circles.

WHISKING WHISKERS

If you look closely as your cat peers into the box, you may see his whiskers swing forward and back. This is called **whisking.** Cats don't see well up close, so they rely on their whiskers to let them know what's right in front of their faces. They also have stiffened hairs just above their eyes and near their ankles. They use information from all of these hairs to decide if an opening is big enough for them to squeeze through. Most cats judge successfully. Their whiskers let them know that their head will fit, and the rest of the body follows suit. The exception is cats who are extremely overweight. They may get their head in and then find that the rest of their body is too big for the opening.

THE SHRINKING CAT

SEE KITTY SLIP THROUGH SMALL PLACES

Cats: If they fit, they sit. Cats across the internet have delighted countless fans by sitting in seemingly too small, oddly shaped spots like vases, tissue boxes, and cupboard drawers. You've probably seen your cat squeezing into some pretty small spaces, too! What's the limit on how small he can get? Use his twin loves of boxes and treats to coax him to show off his shrinking powers.

YOU NEED

Happy Hideaway (p. 20)
treat your cat loves

TIP
After your cat is comfortable going in and out of the box, try making the hole one size smaller. He may be more interested in a tight fit once he is used to the hideaway.

INSTRUCTIONS

1 Set up your happy hideaway with the smallest circle facing outward. Sit next to the hideaway with a treat.

2 Show your cat the treat and let him sniff it. Then put it through the hole into the box.

3 See if your cat follows the treat into the box. If he looks in, but doesn't go through, remove the first paper plate. Now the opening is wider.

4 If needed, show your cat the treat again, and then place it back in the box.

5 Continue removing paper plates until the opening is large enough for your cat to enter and eat the treat.

6 Firmly tape the plate with the right-size hole onto the box so that your cat has a snug hiding place.

 SAFETY NOTE
Do not force your cat to enter the box. If he doesn't want to enter, just leave the box and treat in place. He may choose to enter later.

COLLAPSING COLLARBONE Run your fingers across your shoulder below your neck. Feel that bone? It's your collarbone, also called a clavicle. Your collarbone connects your shoulder to the front of your rib cage, and it limits how tightly you can squeeze your shoulders together. Your cat has a very small collarbone, and it doesn't connect to the front of his rib cage. This allows him to draw his shoulders in very tightly, which leaves his head as the largest body part to squeeze through an opening.

A SIPPING SUBSTITUTE

SEE HOW CATS DRINK

> Difficulty Level:
> **Medium**

> Active Time Needed:
> **20 minutes**

For all her amazing balance and flexibility, there's one thing your cat can't do: sip. The shape of her mouth doesn't allow suction. So when all that activity makes her thirsty, she crouches over her bowl, drags in some water with her tongue, and catches it! How does she do it? Grab a camera and find out.

YOU NEED

shallow glass saucer
can of chicken or tuna
video camera or smartphone
video–editing software or device with slow-motion video capability

INSTRUCTIONS

1 Partially open the can of tuna or chicken and pour the liquid into a saucer.

2 Prepare your phone or camera to record in slow motion.

3 Invite your cat to drink from the saucer. Film her from the side as she drinks, getting as close to her tongue as possible.

4 Watch the film at the slowest speed available and focus on the action of her tongue.

TIP
Most computers and phones come with basic video-editing software that allows video to be slowed after filming. Many will even let you shoot in slo-mo!

ON THE TIP OF HER TONGUE

You may have noticed that your cat bent the tip of her tongue slightly backward and touched it against the surface of the liquid. As she drew her tongue back in, a small column of liquid followed. After a moment, she closed her mouth around the column, catching it.

At the molecular level, water is "sticky." Water molecules are bent, and one side has a slight negative electrical charge. The other side has a slight positive charge. As a result, water molecules cling together—positive end to negative end. They can also stick to other surfaces, such as your cat's tongue. Once one droplet sticks to her tongue, other droplets hang on and come along for the ride. The column rises and thins until gravity takes over and the water falls back into the bowl. Kitty closes her mouth at just the right moment to catch the water before it falls. She can hold the trapped liquid in her mouth for up to 17 licks before she swallows.

Dogs drink in much the same way, with one exception. While cats daintily dip their tongues right at the surface of the water, dogs plunge their tongues all the way into the liquid. So while Fluffy takes a nice, neat sip, Fido splashes water everywhere.

3

TRACKING TABBY

FIGURE OUT YOUR CAT'S FITNESS ROUTINE

> Difficulty Level:
> **Medium**

> Active Time Needed:
> **45 minutes over 5 days**

2

Most people would agree that 4 a.m. is a terrible time to sit on someone's head and purr. And 9 a.m. is a silly time for lazing on top of the computer keyboard. But as you've probably noticed, cats seem to operate on their own schedule. You can use a fitness tracker to uncover what Fluffy is up to when you aren't around. Fitness trackers won't give you her exact number of steps—they count only the movements of her front two legs—but by comparing the number of steps from different times of day, you can see when she is most likely to be up for a romp.

TIP
Make sure to only use a pedometer that is lightweight and isn't irritating for your cat.

YOU NEED

pedometer or other
  fitness tracker
duct tape
zip-top bag or waterproof
  case
cat harness
pencil and paper

TIP
Tape the fitness tracker so that you can see the numbers while your cat is wearing the harness so that you don't have to remove it to record your data.

INSTRUCTIONS

1 Place the pedometer or fitness tracker into the zip-top bag (or case). Fold the extra part of the bag behind the tracker so that you can read the face through the bag.

2 Use duct tape to firmly attach the bag to the cat harness. Make sure to fold the tape so that there are no exposed sticky parts that might pull your cat's hair.

3 If your fitness tracker measures the time of day that your cat is moving, your work is easy. At the end of each day, analyze the data to find out when your kitty was on the move.

4 If you have a simple pedometer, you'll want to check the device periodically. Decide what times of day you will be able to look at the tracker. At each of these times, check the tracker and record the number of steps your kitty has taken. The more times during the day that you can check, the more accurate your data will be.

5 Make a chart showing how many steps she took during each part of the day.

6 Compare the charts to create a schedule for your cat. Which times of day is she most active? When is she reliably resting? Are the times consistent? Or is she busier on some days than others?

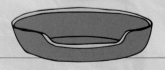

4

TAKE IT FURTHER

Want to know where your outdoor cat goes when she's not with you? Ask an adult for permission and try this experiment with a fitness tracker or watch that gives a GPS reading. When you analyze the data, you can find out if she crosses dangerous streets, has a secret hangout, or might be picking up treats from a neighbor.

6

BASIL'S DAY

5:30–7:00 A.M.	GET UP FOR SOME PLAY AND EAT BREAKFAST.
7:00–8:30 A.M.	FIRST NAP.
8:30–10:30 A.M.	CHECK THE HOUSE OUT AND MAKE SURE NOTHING HAS CHANGED.
10:30 A.M.–3:30 P.M.	NAP NUMBER TWO. THIS ONE IS IMPORTANT.
3:30–6:30 P.M.	MY PEEPS ARE HOME! I MUST FOLLOW THEM AROUND.
6:30–8:00 P.M.	NAP SOME MORE.
8:00 P.M.	QUICK STROLL, THEN BACK TO NAPPING.
8:30 P.M.–1:00 A.M.	MORE NAPPING.
1:00–2:00 A.M.	DO MY PEOPLE NEED TO WAKE UP? GO CHECK.
2:00–5:30 A.M.	ALMOST TIME TO GET UP. BETTER SLEEP SOME MORE TO GET READY.

EVENING ANTICS

Most cats, both house cats and strays, feel friskiest around dawn and dusk. That's when the hunter inside wants to be on the prowl, because that's when many rodents are out and about. Scientists call animals that are on the move at dawn and dusk by a specific name: **crepuscular.** Of course, your data probably indicates that your crepuscular cat is active at other times as well. And research suggests that you have a lot to do with your cat's sleep and awake patterns. Cats that spend the night outside tend to be awake at night. Cats that live indoors are more active during the day, and spend more of their awake-time with their people.

in the LAB

PROSTHETIC PIONEER

Vincent was only a kitten when Mary Sarah Bergh of the Iowa State University College of Veterinary Medicine first met the spunky little tabby. He lay on the examination table, happily licking baby food off a tongue depressor while Bergh examined the place where his hind legs should have been. No one knows what happened to Vincent's hind legs; both were missing below the knee when he was found.

Vincent was adopted by Cindy Jones, who volunteered at the Story County Animal Shelter, where Vincent was brought. Jones fell in love with little Vincent and wanted to help him get around without having to drag his back end.

She took him to Bergh, who was immediately charmed. "He was so vocal," she remembered. "As he licked the baby food he would go 'rawr-rawr-rawr.'"

She evaluated him for legs that could be strapped on, but his left knee had a permanent bend that would prevent a strap from holding. She tried him in a little wheelchair, but he kept flipping it over and falling out. In the meantime, Vincent had developed sores from dragging. Bergh knew there had to be a better solution.

VINCENT SHOWS OFF HIS NEW LEGS.

HIS NEW LEGS LET HIM WALK AND EVEN JUMP!

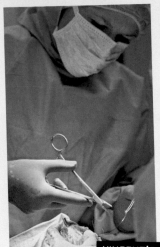
VINCENT'S SURGERY

VINCENT IS ONE HAPPY KITTY!

Prosthetics are helping all kinds of animals. The company that made Vincent's legs has also helped dogs, birds, cows, llamas, and an orangutan!

GOING OUT ON A LIMB

Bergh decided that Vincent's best bet would be implanted **prosthetics:** titanium legs that could attach permanently to his bones. It would require surgery, and the trickiest part would be getting his skin to form a permanent seal where the prosthetics came through. Only a handful of animals around the world had ever been given prosthetics of this kind. They weren't common, even for humans.

Bergh and Jones had watched Vincent stare longingly at adventures that lay just out of reach. He clearly wanted to run around and explore his world. They decided to go for it.

Three years and two surgeries later, Vincent is a marvel. He leaps onto the couch. He goes up and down stairs. He plays with other animals. Vincent's success made Bergh want to help other animals. "He can do everything I ever hoped for him," said Bergh.

GIVING OTHERS A LEG UP

Since Vincent's surgery, Bergh has evaluated many other cats and dogs for prosthetic legs. Most of those animals have been able to use strap-on prosthetic legs, but Bergh has kept careful notes on the techniques she and her team used to help Vincent's skin heal around the implants. She knows there are other animals who would benefit from implants and is excited that Vincent's case might give other cats the freedom to run, walk, and leap into action.

"Vincent let people know what was possible," Bergh said.

CHAPTER 2

SENSATIONAL SENSES

HOW YOUR CAT EXPLORES THE WORLD

Imagine you're a cat, strolling into the living room. Your eye isn't drawn to the big couch or the bold curtains. You don't give the bright painting a second glance. Instead, you home in on the captivating loose thread that's hanging from the recliner and flapping in the breeze. The humans might be playing their so-called music, but you are hearing real music—birdsong coming from the yard. You're also picking up smells that your people have no idea exist: the faint odor emitted by a TV that's turned on, the path where a visitor walked across the carpet last night, the scent of mouse in the wall.

If you were a cat, you'd sense the world very differently. Call your kitty, grab some supplies, and find out more about how the world looks, feels, sounds, tastes, and smells to your favorite feline.

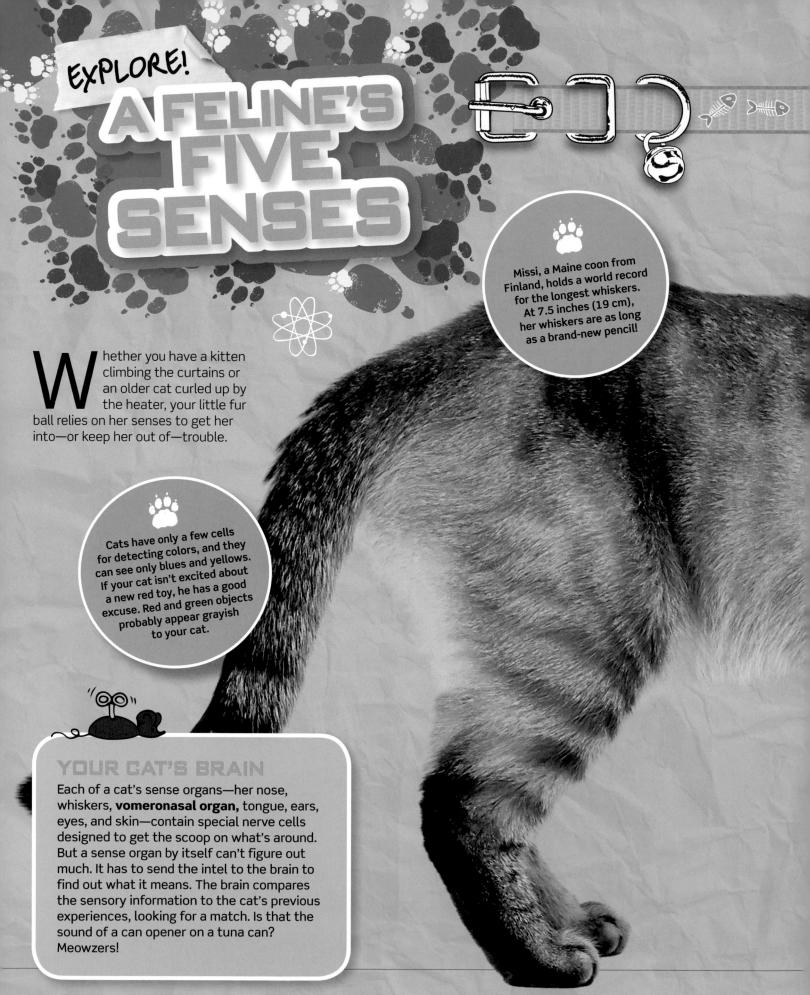

A FELINE'S FIVE SENSES

Missi, a Maine coon from Finland, holds a world record for the longest whiskers. At 7.5 inches (19 cm), her whiskers are as long as a brand-new pencil!

Whether you have a kitten climbing the curtains or an older cat curled up by the heater, your little fur ball relies on her senses to get her into—or keep her out of—trouble.

Cats have only a few cells for detecting colors, and they can see only blues and yellows. If your cat isn't excited about a new red toy, he has a good excuse. Red and green objects probably appear grayish to your cat.

YOUR CAT'S BRAIN

Each of a cat's sense organs—her nose, whiskers, **vomeronasal organ,** tongue, ears, eyes, and skin—contain special nerve cells designed to get the scoop on what's around. But a sense organ by itself can't figure out much. It has to send the intel to the brain to find out what it means. The brain compares the sensory information to the cat's previous experiences, looking for a match. Is that the sound of a can opener on a tuna can? Meowzers!

Nose

It may look small, but the inside of your cat's nose has five times more space devoted to smelling than you do!

Ears

Your cat's ears are like little satellite dishes for sound. They can swivel independently, which lets them locate exactly what direction a sound is coming from.

Whiskers

These long, stiff hairs, also called **vibrissae** (pronounced VEYE-briss-ah), connect to bundles of nerves in Kitty's skin. They alert the brain to everything from a rough jostle to a faint vibration. Your cat's eyes don't focus well up close, so she sweeps her whiskers forward and back to check out the space in front of her face.

Eyes

Kitty's eyes are primed for hunting in the dark. She can use even the dimmest light to see and is especially sensitive to movement. Objects near her face are blurry, though, so she uses other senses to figure out what's going on up close.

Vomeronasal Organ

The vomeronasal organ works like an extra nose. Cats use it specifically for scents released by other cats, called **pheromones**.

Tongue

A cat's tongue is dotted with taste buds that sense the flavors that a meat-eating animal hankers for. Most cats don't care for sweet foods, but some have a fondness for sour.

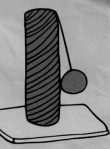

Cats can hear 11 octaves of sound. That's four more sets of do-re-mis than you'll find on a piano.

Leg Vibrissae

Kitty also has whiskers behind her front paws, which help her stay nimble as she hunts in the dark or climbs in treacherous terrain.

TASTE TEST

FIND YOUR CAT'S FAVORITE FLAVORS

> Difficulty Level:
> **Medium**

> Active Time Needed:
> **20 minutes**

It's 6 a.m. and Fluffy is sitting on your head. She's saying it's time for breakfast, whether you like it or not. If you are going to get up, you might as well fill her bowl with food she really likes. Conduct a taste test to see which kibble deserves a nibble.

PICKY, PICKY!

Perhaps your vet recommended a new diet, or perhaps a different brand of cat food was on sale. Either way, many cat owners know the frustration of setting out dinner, only to have Kitty turn up her nose and walk away. Some of the cat's reputation for pickiness comes from the fact that cats have such different food needs from humans'. Cats in the wild eat almost nothing except small animals: mice, birds, lizards, and even insects. Their taste buds are adapted to a pure-carnivore diet—they can't even taste sugar or other sweets.

Being cautious about new foods isn't a bad idea if you're a cat thinking about gobbling a brand-new food. Cats may taste a tiny bit of a new food and wait to see how they feel. Most cats will gradually adjust to a new diet if they are fed the new food often. On the other hand, if your kitty scarfed down both cat foods *and* the dried cranberries, you're not dealing with a picky eater. She'll be happy with any nutritional food you put in her bowl.

TIP
Leave the measuring stick on one side to mark the top of your grid.

1

2

3

TAKE IT FURTHER
Repeat the activity on another day to see if your cat always hankers for the same snacks. Or change out the flavors: Use all canned meats or try several brands of dry treats. Just make sure you keep up with how much you are feeding her, and reduce what you give at mealtime so that she doesn't overeat.

4

YOU NEED

blue painter's tape
9 small paper plates
yardstick or meterstick
2 types of cat food
dried cranberries
pencil and paper

INSTRUCTIONS

1 Prepare the grid. In a clear area, use painter's tape to create a square one yard by one yard (one meter by one meter) wide. Use more tape to divide the square into nine equal boxes, each about one foot (30 cm) wide.

2 Count three pieces of each type of food and three dried cranberries. Place one piece in each square on your grid. Mix it up: Don't put all of the same kinds of food next to each other.

3 Draw the grid on your piece of paper and write down what you put in each square.

4 Just before mealtime, when your cat is hungry, place her in front of the grid. Use your paper to record the order in which she eats the food selections.

5 Review the list. Did she choose one over the others? Were there any she wouldn't eat at all?

NIFTY NIGHT VISION

HOW CATS SEE IN THE DARK

Difficulty Level:
Medium

Active Time Needed:
10 minutes

Big and bright, your cat's distinctive eyes make him pawsitively adorable. And they really are big: Your cat's eyes are almost as big as a person's, but nestled into a much smaller head. Human babies also have eyes that seem too big for their faces, and humans are hardwired to fall for anything adorable like a baby. Your cat, though, isn't just sporting cuteness as a style. His large eyes are perfectly suited to track prey in low light environments. Bring Tiger into a dark room and take a peep at his peepers.

INSTRUCTIONS

1 While your cat is resting in a bright room or in the sun, draw the shape of his eye. Be sure to include the size and shape of the dark black circle in the middle, called the **pupil.**

2 Bring your cat and a flashlight into a dark room. Turn off all the lights and count to 30.

3 Turn on the flashlight and point it toward your paper. Sketch your cat's eye again. Notice the shape and size of his pupil in the dark.

4 Repeat the process to see how your own eye compares. Use the mirror to see the shape of your eye in a bright room and then again in a room that is mostly dark.

YOU NEED

room or closet that you can make dark
flashlight
mirror
pencil and paper

DAYTIME DRAWBACKS

Your eyes and your cat's eyes work in roughly the same way. Light zooms through the pupil and bounces against the **retina.** Then the retina sends the incoming information to the brain. If there's not enough light for the retina to detect, you're stuck fumbling around in the dark. In low light, the pupil stretches wide to capture as much light as possible. And for your cat, that's a big stretch. His pupils can stretch three times as wide as yours, giving him excellent night vision.

He's out of luck on a bright day, however. The retinas get overwhelmed when they are bombarded with too much light. Out in the sun, Kitty's pupils will shrink, but they can't get as small as yours, and they narrow into a slit instead of a dot. You'll notice him squinting so his eyelids will cover the top and bottom of that slit. So while he can see like a champ at dusk and dawn, he doesn't see very clearly in bright sunlight—which makes noon a lovely time for a catnap.

NIGHT STALKING
HUNTING IN THE DARK

> Difficulty Level:
> **Easy**

> Active Time Needed:
> **10 minutes**

Are you afraid of the dark? Your cat's not—that's when the mice come out to play! Cats' eyes are perfectly adapted for hunting in the low light at dawn and dusk, exactly the time that most rodents are on the move. Cats can't see in complete darkness, but they need only a bit of light to spot their prey. Find out how little illumination is needed for your cat to go on the hunt.

YOU NEED

room or closet that you can make dark
flashlight
3–4 feathers
masking tape
string

INSTRUCTIONS

1 Tape the feathers together in a bundle by the tips. Cut a piece of string about two feet (0.6 m) long, and tie it to the bundle of feathers.

2 Invite your cat back into the dark room. Make the room as dark as possible.

3 Give your cat about one minute to adjust to the darkness, then bounce the feather bundle around on the string, as quietly as possible! If your cat can see the toy, you will feel a tug on the string when he pounces on it.

4 If he doesn't respond, try letting in a small amount of light by shining a flashlight in the corner of the room or turning on a light outside so that a little comes under the door. Bounce the toy again.

5 Continue adding light until your cat can see enough to hunt. How much light does he need?

THAT GREEN GLOW

It's so hard to get a photograph of little Tiger without capturing a devilish glare in his eyes. That green glow comes from an eye structure that can compete with night-vision goggles. For your cat to see, light must enter his eye and land on a thin film of cells called the retina. Behind the retina is a layer of tissue called the **tapetum.** The tapetum works like a mirror. Any light that misses the retina on the first pass hits the tapetum and bounces back, giving the retina another shot at capturing it. Some of the rebounding light comes back out through the pupil and shows up in your photo as an eerie green glow.

The retina has two kinds of cells. Rod cells detect motion, even in low light. Cone cells sense color but need a lot of light to work. Because of this, your cat has amazing night vision, but he sees everything in black and white.

HEAR THAT?

LISTEN LIKE A CAT

Difficulty Level:
Easy

Active Time Needed:
10 minutes

Your cat can hear a rumble of thunder so deep that it would pass your ear undetected. She can hear the high-pitched squeak of a mouse that would be as silent as a dog whistle to you. She can hear high and low and everything in between. With all that sound surrounding her, what does she pay attention to? Try some recordings to find out what's music to her ears.

YOU NEED

device with speakers (e.g., a phone, device connected to a Bluetooth speaker, or computer)
sound clip of a songbird that is local to your area
sound clip of a songbird that does not live in your area
sound clip of a squirrel chittering
clip of your favorite music

INSTRUCTIONS

1 Do some research on bird species in your area. Ask an adult to help you research online and find sound clips of the calls for one of your local birds and one that is not native to your area.

2 Prepare the bird, squirrel, and music sound clips on your phone or computer so that you can easily switch between sounds.

3 Draw a chart like the one below to record your observations.

4 Select a time when your cat is resting. Place your speaker behind her and several feet away.

5 Play 10 seconds of your favorite music at a comfortable listening level. Use your chart to record her reactions: Do her ears move? Does she turn her head toward the sound? Does she get up to search for the sound, or run away from it?

6 Wait one minute for her to resume resting.

7 Play 10 seconds of the sound of a local bird chirping (the bird sounds will likely start and stop a few times during that period, which is OK). Record her reactions.

8 Wait at least one minute for her to resume resting, and then repeat with 10 seconds of the clip of a bird that doesn't live in your area. Record her reactions.

9 Repeat the test with the sound of a squirrel chittering.

10 Test each sound three times. Which sounds got the most reaction? Did any of them get her up and ready to hunt?

	MUSIC	LOCAL BIRDSONG	NONLOCAL BIRDSONG	SQUIRREL CHIRRUP
EAR MOVEMENT?				
TURN HEAD TOWARD SOUND?				
GET UP AND MOVE TOWARD OR AWAY FROM THE SOUND?				

5

TAKE IT FURTHER

Scientists at the University of Wisconsin–Madison and musicians at the University of Maryland have developed music to appeal specifically to cats. It includes many high-pitched notes along with the rhythms of purring. With the help of a parent, head to *musicforcats.com* and see if your cat is ready to head to a kitty concert. Or try other sounds, such as big cats roaring, kittens mewing, or another cat purring.

A HUNTER'S HEARING

Chirp! A sound ripples through the air toward your cat. Her first move comes from the ears, which swivel to capture the sound. Her external ears, called **pinnae,** funnel the sound into her ear canal, where it hits the eardrum. The eardrum passes the vibrations into her inner ear, where they reach a series of hairlike cells. Each hair is tuned to a different pitch, and when they shake, they trigger a nerve cell to send a message to the brain. It's a bird, brain!

Dogs get all the glory for having amazing hearing, but cats hear vibrations both lower and higher than dogs. They can even hear the ultrasonic peeps that bats use to find their way in the dark. Hearing is critical on the hunt. Cats usually first locate their prey by sound. They are especially sensitive to the squeaks that rodents use to communicate and the scratching sounds of mouse feet on the run.

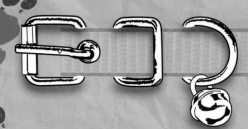

THE PURRFECT MOOD

FIND OUT WHAT GETS YOUR CAT PURRING

> **Difficulty Level:**
> **Easy**

> **Active Time Needed:**
> **10 minutes**

Snuggle with your cat on the sofa (if she's in the mood!), and in minutes, you'll hear and feel the gentle rumble of her purr. Not only is this purr a wonderful way to win your affection (after all, who doesn't love the comfort-ng sound of a purr?), it's a pretty neat physical trick as well. Cats purr when they exhale and when they inhale. That's no small accomplishment—try calling "good kitty" while breathing in. To top it off, purring takes place at an amazingly deep pitch—lower than the lowest key on a piano. Try these activities to find out exactly what it takes to get your kitty's motor rumbling.

YOU NEED

cat-size stuffed animal
recording of a cat purr (available online)
bowl of your cat's food

P-P-P-P-PURR!

Gently stroke your cat along her throat. Feel that stiff spot? That's her voice box, or larynx. The larynx is made of several plates of stiff cartilage. Inside, there are two skin-like flaps called vocal cords. When a cat purrs, she sends a stream of air through the vocal cords. At the same time, the vocal cords open and close rapidly, turning that air in a series of puffs. You can make a similar sound by shaping your lips to make the sound of the letter *p*. Now blow out, while making the *p* sound over and over. If you could repeat the *p* sound 25 times in a single second, you'd have something like a purr.

VOCAL CORD

LARYNX

INSTRUCTIONS

1 Pick a time when your cat is calm but awake. Most cats will purr when they are relaxed and being petted. Pet your cat for one minute and time how much of the minute she spends purring. If she does not purr, wait until another time to do this experiment.

2 Now that you know she is in the mood to purr, you can try other things that might inspire her. Gently place the cat-size stuffed animal against your cat's back. Time for one minute and write down how much time she spends purring.

3 Play the sound of another cat purring for one minute. Record how much of the time she purrs.

4 Is your presence enough to make her purr? Sit next to, without touching, your cat for one minute, and record her purring time.

5 Go to the place where you usually prepare your cat's meals. Follow the steps you usually take (open the food, pick up her bowl, etc.). If your cat comes to her feeding place, observe whether she is purring and record the time for one minute.

6 Compare the amount of time she spent purring with each situation. What gets her in a *purr*fect mood?

TAKE IT FURTHER

Find out exactly how deep your cat's purr is. Grab an electronic tuner or, with an adult's permission, download a tuning app. As she purrs, place the tuner just in front of her mouth and nose, where the purr sound is loudest. Look for the measurement of the pitch in hertz (Hz). Your tuner may also tell you the name of the note closest to the pitch your cat is producing. Try the tuner on yourself. Can you make a sound that is deeper than your cat's purr?

WHAT DOES A PURR MEAN?

Cats purr to each other and to us, but it's not clear what cats are saying when they purr. Most of the time, it seems to show that they are content. Kittens start purring when they are only a few days old, and purr when they are nursing. But cats also purr when they are sick or in pain—but only if another cat or human is around. Clearly, purring is intended to communicate important messages to those nearby. Whatever the message may be, that deep, rumbly purr feels close and cuddly.

FEATHER FLIER

MAKE A TERRIFIC TOY FOR YOUR KITTY

> Difficulty Level:
> **Easy**

> Active Time Needed:
> **15 minutes**

What's that? A bird? A new sock to destroy? No, it's the fantastic feather flier! Playful kitties like fluffy feathers and toys that move. Put the two together with this feather flier. Make it even more alluring by finding the perfect scent to add to it with "Awesome Odors" on p. 42.

YOU NEED

plastic clothes hanger
yarn or string
tape
permanent marker
4 small binder clips
   or clothespins
craft feathers
safety scissors

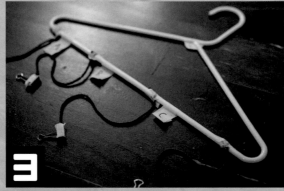

5

INSTRUCTIONS

1 Cut four pieces of yarn or string, each about six inches (15 cm) long.

2 Tie the strings at equal intervals across the bar of the hanger. Tape the knots in place so they do not slide around when your kitty plays with the toy.

3 Use the permanent marker to label the strings A, B, C, and D.

4 Tie the other end of each piece of string to a binder clip or clothespin. Clip a feather to each one.

5 Hang the hanger on the edge of a table or a doorknob and give it a little push to make the feathers fly.

⚠ SAFETY NOTE
Make sure all of the sticky edges of tape are pressed down firmly so there is no exposed adhesive that might catch on Kitty's fur.

SCAREDY-CATS Many cats will flee from the vacuum cleaner, but some cats are frightened of every new thing that comes through the door. If you've got one of these fraidy-cats, he might not be eager to play with his new feather flier. Try leaving it hanging in place for a while until your cat can build up the nerve to check it out. Research suggests that your presence can also help. When cats encounter a new object, they often look to their owner's reaction to the object to determine if it is safe. In one study, when owners looked pleased with a new object and spoke to their cats encouragingly, the cats were more likely to approach the item than when the owners looked upset and spoke with a warning tone of voice.

AWESOME ODORS

DISCOVER YOUR CAT'S FAVORITE SMELLS

> Difficulty Level:
> **Easy**

> Active Time Needed:
> **5 minutes**

Outside, a cat's nose is bombarded by odors: fresh-cut grass, face oils from the cat next door, a delightful trickle of mouse pee. Inside, the smells can become a little ho-hum. Tigers, cheetahs, cougars, and other cats kept in zoos have similar problems with boredom. Zookeepers have figured out that unusual scents can distract the cats. Big cats sometimes respond to cinnamon, cumin, chili powder, and perfumes. Tigers are especially fond of one popular brand of cologne. Use your feather flier (p. 40) or a similar toy from your cat's collection to find scents that will bring out the tiger hidden in your kitty.

YOU NEED

feather flier
scent sources, including perfumes
    or colognes, or spices such as
    cinnamon, chili powder, or cumin
pencil and paper
timer or clock

SCENT-ILLATING SMELLS

Take a deep breath, drawing air in through your nose. On its way to the lungs, the air races past your scent detection cells. You have several million of them, crammed into a space about the size of a postage stamp. If that sounds like a lot, consider that your cat has a whopping 200 million scent detectors! They are packed into her **olfactory membrane,** or scent detection area, which is five times as large as yours. For all of that olfactory membrane to fit inside her tiny nose, it is rippled and folded throughout the air passage.

When you breathe out, any smells you haven't noticed zip right back out with your breath. Your cat can process smells at a more leisurely pace. When she inhales, she can send some of the air into a pocket at the top of her nose. The air stays trapped until she has all the odor information she needs from it. Meanwhile, she can continue to breathe in and out normally.

TAKE IT FURTHER

Repeat the experiment several times. Is she attracted to the same smells each time? It's also possible that your cat prefers the location of a feather on the feather flier rather than a specific smell. As you repeat the experiment, change the location of the odors. Try new odors (on fresh feathers) until you find some that your cat seems to enjoy. Try rubbing those smells on other cat toys around the house. Does your cat show new interest in the scented toys?

INSTRUCTIONS

1 Select three odors to test. Dip the end of a feather into one of the odor sources and then clip the feather to one of the clips on your feather flier. Write down which string (A, B, C, or D) you clipped it to.

2 Repeat for the other two odors. Leave one feather with no scent as a control group.

3 Hang the hanger near your cat and wait until she approaches. If she ignores the new toy, try tapping the edge of the hanger so the feathers shake.

4 Time how long she sniffs or plays with each feather before moving on. If she returns to a feather, record that as well.

5 Continue timing until she gets bored and wanders off.

6 Compare the times. Did she spend more time with a specific scent? Or did she prefer the unscented control feather?

TIP

It takes only a tiny amount of the smelly substance to do the job. Your cat's sense of smell is so sensitive that she can be overwhelmed by a strong scent.

2

3

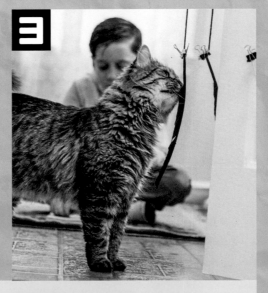

4

⚠ SAFETY NOTE

Don't use odors from substances that are not good for cats, such as chocolate, onions, or garlic. Make sure you grab an adult and carefully research each item you decide to use.

in the LAB

TERRIFIC TONGUES

Alexis Noel's fascination with cat tongues started with a visit to her parents' house. She was home on holiday from the Georgia Institute of Technology, where she was studying how frog tongues help them capture flies.

She had just settled into a chair, tucked under a blanket, when Murphy, her parents' four-year-old tabby, leaped into her lap. He began to lick, and in moments, his tongue was stuck.

"Can you imagine this cat with this blanket sticking out of his mouth?" Noel remembers, laughing and sticking her own tongue out and flapping it hopelessly like the cat. "So I helped him detangle the blanket from his tongue. And I was like—huh. That's kind of interesting."

It just happened that Alexis was about to expand her research into different types of tongues, and was looking for a new licking apparatus to explore. Murphy's mishap made her next target obvious: What kind of tongue could stick to a blanket?

If a cat worked steadily from tail to nose, it would take about one hour for her to fully groom herself.

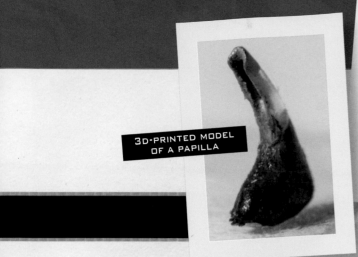

3D-PRINTED MODEL OF A PAPILLA

PAPILLAE ON A CAT TONGUE LIE IN ROWS.

A Spiky Licker

She started looking at cat tongues: house cats, bobcats, snow leopards, tigers, and more. All of these cats have tiny spines, called **papillae,** coating their tongues. The spines are shaped like cat claws, each as thin as a sewing needle; they lie in rows with their tips pointing toward the throat. When a cat extends his tongue to lick, the spines lift up, creating a row of bristles like a hairbrush. But not just any hairbrush. Using 3D-printed models of cat tongues, Noel studied how these spines work for grooming. She found that the shape and flexibility of the spines allow them to pull through tangles more easily than a human hairbrush.

Cats also use their tongues to scrape meat from bones. So Noel picked up a pork chop and headed to the lab to test "licks" using a preserved cat tongue. The tongue easily scooped off the meat. But to her surprise, the meat did not wash off easily afterward. She found the reason under a high-powered microscope—the papillae had a hollow groove on the underside that no one had noticed before.

Further research showed that this groove fills with cat spit, which works like a detangling spray. When a cat grooms himself, each lick delivers a tongue-full of detangler right to the base of his hairs. The system is so remarkable that Noel hopes to use the cat tongue as a blueprint for a better human hairbrush.

Detangling spit has a downside: People who are allergic to cats are usually allergic to their spit, not their fur.

Thanks, Murphy!

Noel also knows to keep Murphy away from that microfiber blanket! Microfiber is made of loops of very strong thread. While a cat's licking apparatus is great for muscling through tough tangles, it's no match for the strength of microfiber. Instead, Noel gives him extra-special snuggles and thanks him for giving her an unusual introduction to cat tongues.

BEWARE OF MICROFIBER!

CHAPTER 3

PURRFECT PREDATORS

HOW YOUR CAT HUNTS

The cat slowly stalks across his territory. His tail twitches in concentration. As he moves, the muscles ripple under his skin and he never blinks. Then—POUNCE! Is it a tiger chasing a wild boar? No—it's a house cat stalking a loose shoelace!

Cats haven't lived with people for as long as dogs have. And people haven't bred them to do chores, the way we did with dogs. So in many ways, domestic cats are only a few steps away from their wild cousins. Even though your cat has a bowl of food at the ready, he still wants to protect his territory and practice his hunting.

Give him a chance to do both with the activities in this chapter.

MINE, ALL MINE!

She rubs against your legs, the corner in the hallway, and the edge of the couch. She bumps her forehead against your knee. But why? Your cat has nine types of odor **glands** distributed around her body, and all that rubbing spreads her scent. Some scientists would say she's claiming you. Others suspect she is creating a blend of her smell and yours, to show that you belong together.

GETTING THE MESSAGE

To humans, it's a smelly mess, but to felines, it's a treasure trove of information. How do cats read all of this info that other cats have left around? They use their **vomeronasal organ,** a sense organ dedicated to smelling just one thing—other cats. The opening to the vomeronasal organ is on the roof of a cat's mouth, behind his front teeth. To get the air in, a cat holds his mouth slightly open, breathes in, and directs the air up with his tongue. Sometimes you can hear a little huffing sound as he works. His expression looks a bit like a grimace, and scientists call this face the **flehmen response.** Cats will flehmen in response to meeting a new cat, finding cat urine, or locating places where other cats have rubbed against walls or trees. What are they learning from all this huffing and puffing? Information about who has been in their territory, whether a neighbor cat is ready to mate, and how strong their rivals may be. It's better to sniff out that sort of information than learn it in a catfight.

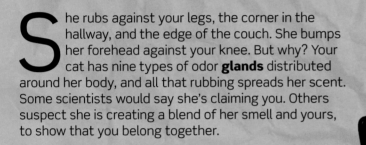

PERIORAL GLANDS:

With these glands at the sides of her mouth, Kitty can add her scent to whatever she decides merits a little chew.

The stinky chemical in male cat urine is similar to a chemical in garlic, which is why they both have such a strong smell.

CAUDAL AND SUPRACAUDAL GLANDS:

These glands throughout the tail allow your cat to mark her territory with her back end as well as her front.

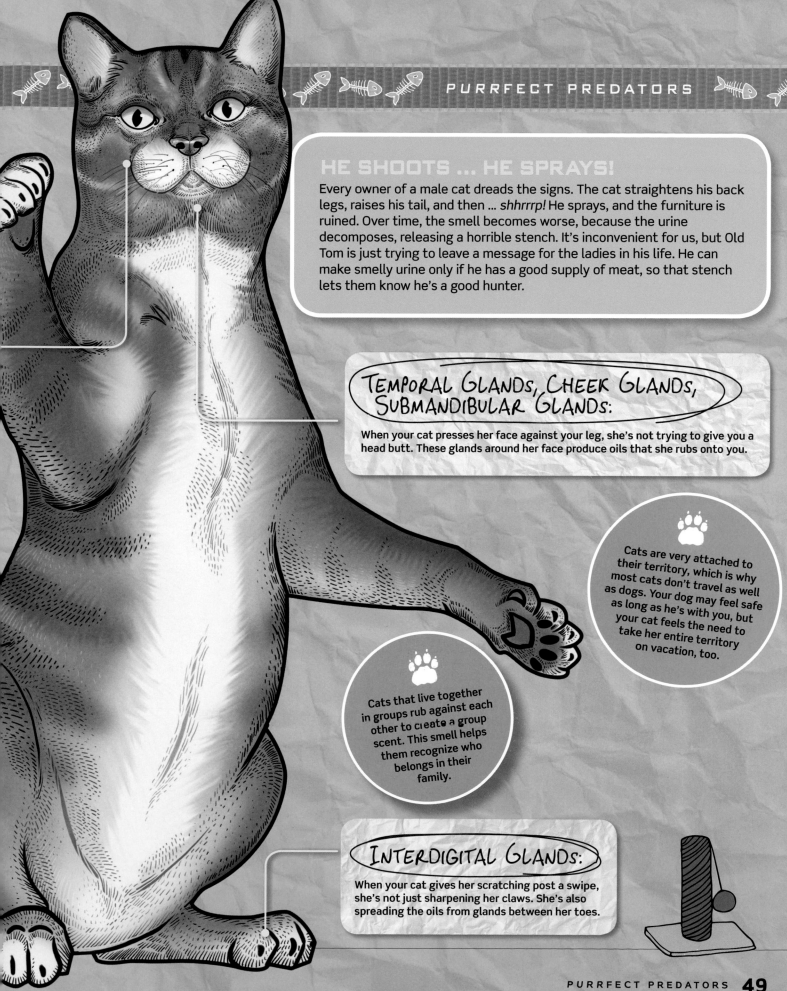

HE SHOOTS ... HE SPRAYS!

Every owner of a male cat dreads the signs. The cat straightens his back legs, raises his tail, and then ... *shhrrrp!* He sprays, and the furniture is ruined. Over time, the smell becomes worse, because the urine decomposes, releasing a horrible stench. It's inconvenient for us, but Old Tom is just trying to leave a message for the ladies in his life. He can make smelly urine only if he has a good supply of meat, so that stench lets them know he's a good hunter.

TEMPORAL GLANDS, CHEEK GLANDS, SUBMANDIBULAR GLANDS:

When your cat presses her face against your leg, she's not trying to give you a head butt. These glands around her face produce oils that she rubs onto you.

Cats are very attached to their territory, which is why most cats don't travel as well as dogs. Your dog may feel safe as long as he's with you, but your cat feels the need to take her entire territory on vacation, too.

Cats that live together in groups rub against each other to create a group scent. This smell helps them recognize who belongs in their family.

INTERDIGITAL GLANDS:

When your cat gives her scratching post a swipe, she's not just sharpening her claws. She's also spreading the oils from glands between her toes.

TERRITORY CHANGE-UP

DISCOVER YOUR CAT'S TERRITORIAL NATURE

> Difficulty Level:
> **Medium**

> Active Time Needed:
> **30 minutes**

You know the comfy armchair in the living room you always sit in? Well, according to your cat, he owns it. He just lets you use it! Your cat has staked out his territory and keeps a close watch over everything that happens there. Find out how closely he observes his dominion by making a small change and watching to see if he notices.

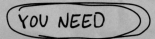

YOU NEED

permission to move furniture and artwork

INSTRUCTIONS

1 Select a room where your cat spends a lot of time. Draw a map of the room. Include doors, windows, furniture, artwork, throw pillows, stacks of books, or any other features that are always in the room.

2 Observe your cat in the room for 15 minutes. Note where he spends his time and what furniture and objects he interacts with.

3 Close the room so that your cat cannot enter while you find five to seven ways to change the room. Shift at least one piece of furniture 6–12 inches (15–30 cm). Consider moving a lamp, changing the location of artwork, and rearranging items that have been in the same location for a long time. Mark your changes on the map.

4 Bring your cat into the room. He won't tell you if he notices that things are different, so you will have to look for clues in his body language.

5 Observe his behavior for 15 minutes and again record where he spends his time and what he interacts with. Look for any unusual behaviors, such as sniffing objects that he usually ignores or spending extra time rubbing against furniture that has been moved. He may look to you to see if any of the changes trouble you.

1

TIP
To decide what furniture to move, get down to the floor to see what might be important from a cat's-eye view.

2

3

4

DON'T TOUCH MY TURF!

So you already knew that your cat likes to act like a queen, but did you know that she really rules her own space? Cats are very attached to the places where they live. Most cats have **territory,** or a small area to control and defend from other cats. Then they have a larger home range—all of the spaces they may wander in the course of their day. For cats that live indoors, their territory may be about the same as their home range. Or maybe not! Cats who live together may divide the house up, with different areas serving as the territory of the different cats. If you have multiple cats, you may be able to observe where they sleep to figure out which areas are claimed by which kitty.

Cats who go outdoors have more variation in their territory and home range. One study found that the most extreme adventurers traveled distances greater than 10 city blocks from their houses. But many cats are homebodies. In another study, most cats stayed within 100 yards (91 m) of their houses, and some didn't even venture a full 25 feet (8 m) away from their cat flap. That's less than the length of a school bus!

Keeping tabs on her territory makes your cat feel secure. When something changes, like when furniture moves around, she may express surprise by paying extra attention to the furniture, marking it with the **glands** on her face, or trying to attract your attention to the change by crouching or jumping at the furniture.

PLAYING CAT AND MOUSE

INVESTIGATING PREY SIZE

> Difficulty Level:
> **Easy**

> Active Time Needed:
> **30 minutes**

If you're going to do science with your cat, it should involve at least one lab rat. Fortunately, for this activity, you won't have to use a real one! Scientists have observed that cats hunt rats and mice using different methods, and the difference seems to be related to the size of the prey. Make a mouse-size toy and a rat-size toy and see if your cat likes to take on the big guys.

YOU NEED

yarn or string
3 sheets of tissue paper
timer

INSTRUCTIONS

1 For the mouse-size toy, use one sheet of tissue paper to make a wad about the size of a lemon. Loosen one edge of the wad and tear a two- to three-inch (5- to 7-cm) strip, leaving one end attached. This gives the toy a "tail." Tie a piece of string around the middle of your mouse so you can make it move.

2 For the rat-size toy, stack two pieces of tissue paper together and make a wad about the size of a large baking potato. Once again, loosen an edge and tear a tail. Tie a string around the middle.

3 Time to play cat-and-mouse! Set your timer for two minutes. Slowly drag the mouse-size toy across the floor in front of your cat. Does she pounce? If so, observe which body parts she attacks with—her teeth, front legs, back legs? Continue pulling the toy back and forth and record how many times she pounces in the two-minute period.

4 Now for your lab rat. Set the timer for another two minutes and pull the rat-size toy across the floor. Record how many times your cat pounces. If your cat attacks, observe which parts of her body she uses.

THIS HUNTER IS NOT KITTEN AROUND!

Did your cat tackle the bigger prey? Researchers have found that more cats will take on a mouse-size toy than a rat-size toy. In real life, a rat is formidable prey. It has sharp teeth and is strong enough to injure a cat. Cats who take on rat-size toys use their teeth and all four legs, kicking the toy with their hind legs, just as a cat would when attacking a real rat.

If your cat goes for bigger prey, chances are good that she was born to a mother who hunted her own food. While cats are born with an instinct to chase prey, they are taught hunting skills by their mother during their first year of life. As she **weans** them off milk, she brings them prey. At first, the prey is dead. But once they are comfortable eating it, she captures live prey so they can practice attacking. Indeed, it is possible that when your cat brings you a creature that she has caught, she is thinking of you as a kitten who needs to learn to hunt!

HUNGRY HUNTER

HOW HUNGER AFFECTS PLAY

Sometimes you wave a feather, and your cat leaps right into hunting mode. Other times, your cat gives you a bored stare and goes back to grooming. What gives? Try inviting her to play before and after eating to see how hunger affects playfulness.

TIP
For the most accurate results, do the tests several times over several days—playing before the meal on some days and after the meal on others.

YOU NEED

3 cat toys
watch or timer
paper and pencil

INSTRUCTIONS

1 About 10 minutes before her normal mealtime, sit near your cat and wiggle one of the toys. Continue to move the toy around for one minute. Record how much of the minute she spends playing with you.

2 Change toys and record how much of a minute she spends playing with this toy. Spend one more minute offering her a third toy.

3 Feed your cat her usual meal. Let her eat as much as she wants, and do not disturb her until she leaves the food bowl on her own.

4 Sit near her and offer the three toys again, each for one minute. Record how long she plays with each toy.

PLAYFUL SCIENCE

Cats have a reputation for quickly tiring of their toys. Are they truly that picky? Or do we just not understand what they like? Researchers have been teasing out what makes fabulous play for a cat and have found, as you might expect, that it's closely related to hunting. The same factors that cause a cat to go on the prowl can also put her in the mood to play. Cats are more likely to play when they are hungry. They'll choose toys that resemble their prey: toys covered with fur or feathers, or with many legs, like a spider. They play the longest with toys that change as they play with them, by ripping or shredding. If play is like hunting, then that tough toy that doesn't break down might be prey that is too difficult to conquer.

MOUSE HIDEOUT

BUILD A HIDING SPOT FOR YOUR KITTY'S TOYS

> **Difficulty Level:**
> **Easy**

> **Active Time Needed:**
> **25 minutes**

For a cat, any good hunt involves flushing the prey out of hiding. Liven up the games with your cat by creating a hiding spot where your cat's toys can "retreat." Add a twist by creating two different dens, so your cat has to watch closely to know where to go.

YOU NEED

2 sheets of poster board
wide tape (such as packing tape or duct tape)

INSTRUCTIONS

1 Fold both sheets of poster board in half, across the long side.

2 Lay the folded sides next to each other and tape them together securely. Flip the posters over and tape them on the back side as well.

3 Take one loose edge of the board and fold it backward until it meets the center fold. Repeat with the top loose edge on the other poster board.

4 Flip the entire thing over. Fold those loose edges toward the center.

5 Set the posters on the ground and arrange the folds to create two compartments with small side openings.

1

2

TIP
When cats are hunting, they sometimes head straight for their target. Other times, they slink along an indirect route, as if they're trying to confuse the mouse into running in the wrong direction.

TIP
You can use this apparatus to hide toys and treats for your cat to find, and to complete "Where's My Mouse?" (p. 56).

4

WHERE'S MY MOUSE?

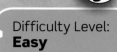

TEST YOUR CAT'S MEMORY

> Difficulty Level:
> **Easy**

> Active Time Needed:
> **10 minutes**

Imagine you're hunting a mouse. Suddenly, the quick critter disappears down a hole. You can't see it, but you know it still exists, right? Does your cat? It's a question that scientists have been asking cats through a variety of experiments over the last 50 years. These researchers want to know if cats understand **object permanence,** or the fact that something can still exist even if they can't see it or feel it. It's one way of finding out how "smart" an animal is. Human babies grasp object permanence by about 10 months old. Is your cat as smart as a 10-month-old? Try this activity to find out.

TIP
Slide your prey into the den while your cat is stalking, but before she starts to pounce.

YOU NEED

mouse hideout
    (see p. 54 to make one)
toy mouse or other toy on
    a string that is at least
    two feet (0.6 m) long

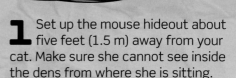

1

2

INSTRUCTIONS

1 Set up the mouse hideout about five feet (1.5 m) away from your cat. Make sure she cannot see inside the dens from where she is sitting.

2 Place the toy or treat near your cat and wiggle the string until your cat begins to watch with interest or paw at the toy.

3 As your cat watches, pull the pretend prey into one of the dens and drop the string.

4 Step back. When your cat comes after the pretend prey, does she know which den to look in?

5 Repeat the experiment but hide the prey in the other den and see if your cat notices the change and looks there. Continue until your cat gets bored, periodically changing the den where the prey hides.

GONE BUT NOT FORGOTTEN

In studies, most cats (those feeling cooperative enough to participate) have no trouble understanding that the missing prey still exists behind a barrier. In fact, when scientists used a screen to hide the prey from view just before it ran behind a barrier, cats could still guess that the prey would be behind the barrier closest to where it disappeared. This shows the cats remembered that the prey existed and that they maintained a mental picture of the scene of the hunt. But your cat is no Einstein. His memory only lasts a few seconds. By the time a minute has passed, he'll have moved on to other things.

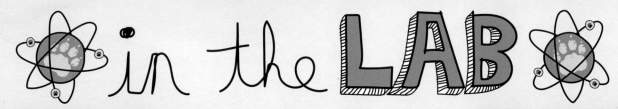

in the LAB

CAUGHT ON CRITTERCAM

Kyler Abernathy, director of research for the Exploration Technology Lab at the National Geographic Society, is in the business of finding out what animals are up to when we can't see them. He and his team build video recording systems called Crittercams for animals to wear as they go about their day. Abernathy's team has used them with more than 80 species of animals, helping scientists see the secret lives of seals, sea turtles, buffalo, bears, elephants, squid, and more. Recently Abernathy and the National Geographic Crittercam team turned their cameras on cats.

CARRYING THE CAMERA

THE VIEW THROUGH A CRITTERCAM

SMALL CAMERAS FOR SMALL ANIMALS

Abernathy's first cat experiment came about by chance. He was working on a new camera system and needed something to try it out on. A neighbor had four cats who were always leaving "gifts" of dead rodents on the porch. Abernathy could try out his new system, and the neighbor could find out what else his cats were getting into.

The challenge was rigging up a camera that cats could comfortably carry. Cats are smaller than many of the other animals that Abernathy had worked with, so he needed a device that was smaller as well.

He ordered a tiny camera and attached it to a custom micro-controller, and then added a battery. He put the whole thing in a small plastic container, sealed it up, and attached it to a cat harness.

After tracking the cats for several nights, he came back to his neighbor with some interesting news. Only one of the cats was a hunter. The other three didn't catch anything at all. But the hunting cat was killing and eating one to two extra animals for every one she brought home. Abernathy wondered what other secrets cats might be keeping.

ON THE HUNT

TOO BIG TO TACKLE!

The average adult male cat weighs about seven pounds (3.2 kg). The average female weighs about a pound (.45 kg) less.

THE SECRET LIVES OF CATS

A few years later, Abernathy was contacted by researchers from the University of Georgia who wanted to do a bigger study. Many people are concerned about how cat hunting may impact other species. It's hard to know how big the problem is, because researchers have only been able to count the prey that cats bring home. If the cats wore cameras, the researchers could see exactly what was killed.

Out of 55 cats who wore the cameras for a week, less than half did any hunting at all. But like Abernathy's neighbor's cat, the hunters could be quite deadly. Together, the hunting cats killed 39 small animals. Abernathy said the biggest surprise was the variety of the prey. "People think about the birds," he said, but the most common prey were lizards, and cats chose widely from worms to voles to insects to chipmunks. In total, only five of the dead animals were birds.

Four cats in the Crittercam project had "second families" they liked to visit.

A second surprise was how many times the videos showed the cats doing something dangerous. Almost half crossed roads, and a fifth of the cats went down into storm drains, where they risked drowning or getting trapped. They also ate and drank unknown substances, met up with other cats, and one even crawled into a car engine.

The team hadn't intended to study risks for outdoor cats, but that's the advantage of using Crittercams. "We often find answers to questions we hadn't even known to ask when we started," said Abernathy. The videos "are such a detailed source of data. We can see not just where the animal is, but what it is doing, and what else is nearby."

Abernathy hopes the findings from this study will cause people to rethink how often their cats go outside, for the sake of wildlife and for their cat's safety.

A BIRD ESCAPES.

TIME FOR DINNER?

CHAPTER 4

CLEVER KITTIES

INSIDE THE MINDS OF CATS

Cats are a mystery. One moment, they want nothing to do with you, and the next, they're pawing at the door trying to join you in the bathroom. They love a good roll all over the math homework you are trying to finish. And what's with repeatedly knocking all of the pencils off your desk? You wonder what on Earth is going through her mind! You aren't the only one. Scientists are researching how cats learn and think, what makes cats happy, and which personality traits are common in cats. In the past, cats haven't gotten as much attention from researchers as dogs, but that's changing. Scientists around the world are now sifting through the mysteries of the cat brain.

Call for Kitty and turn the page to delve into the science of cat cognition.

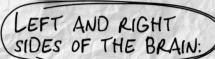

EXPLORE!
PEEK INTO THE BRAIN

LEFT AND RIGHT SIDES OF THE BRAIN:

Your kitty's thinker is divided into two halves, called **hemispheres**. The left hemisphere controls the right side of his body, and his right hemisphere controls the left side.

You can almost see Tiger thinking as he gets ready to pounce. If only you could uncover the thoughts zipping around his brain. Scientists can't do that yet, but they know a lot about your cat's thinking machine.

CEREBRUM:

You've closed the door to the bathroom, but your cat is determined to find a way in. You can bet his cerebrum is hard at work. The cerebrum is the folded, twisty layer that makes the brain look like a plate of spaghetti. The cerebrum handles learning, memory, and decision-making, and processes information sent in from the sensory organs.

HOW DO YOU TEST A TABBY'S INTELLIGENCE?

There are many ways for Fluffy to show her genius, but one common test given by psychologists is a string-pulling test that shows whether animals understand cause and effect. In this task, a string with a treat tied to the end is placed under a clear box. The animals are taught how to pull the string to get the food. Then they are given a box with two strings. One is tied to a piece of food. The other isn't tied to anything. If the animals understand cause and effect, they should look at the two strings and then pull the one attached to the treat. Dogs can pass the string test, as can monkeys, raccoons, and a whole bunch of bird species. But when scientists gave the string-pulling test to cats, the cats pulled the wrong string as often as the right one, which suggests they didn't understand the relationship between the treat and the string. Or did they? One researcher in a recent string-pulling test suggested that perhaps the cats weren't motivated by the treats. They just enjoyed pulling the strings!

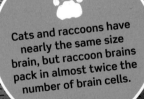

Cats and raccoons have nearly the same size brain, but raccoon brains pack in almost twice the number of brain cells.

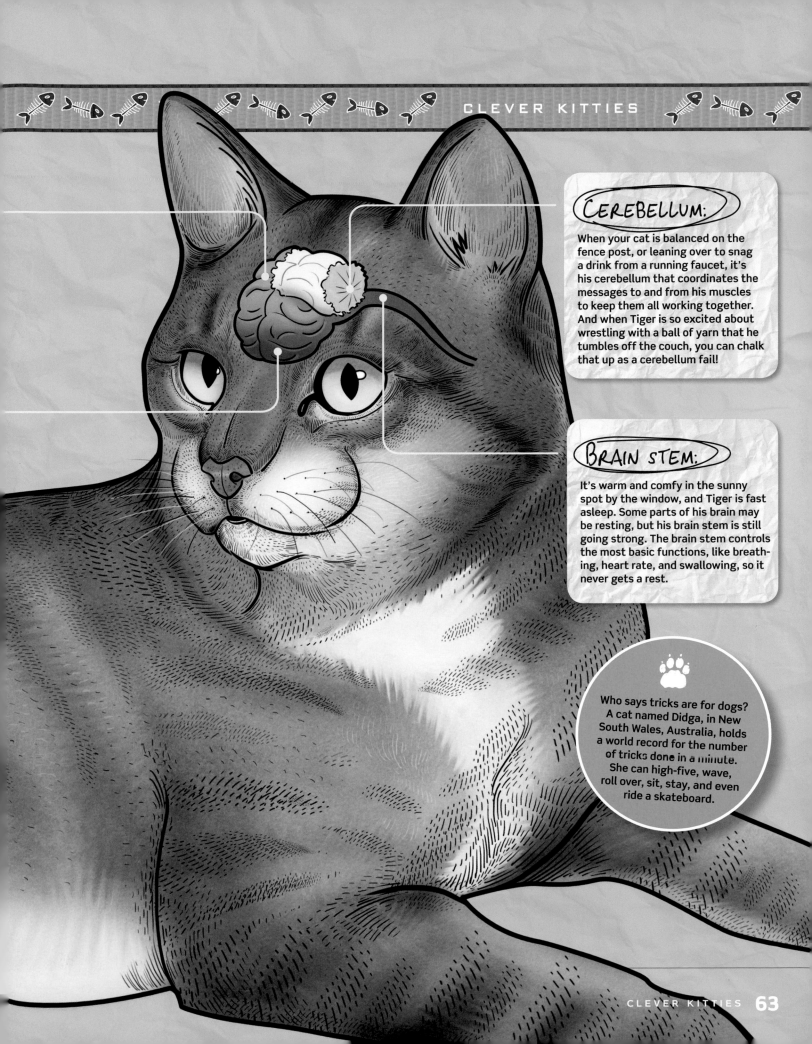

CEREBELLUM:

When your cat is balanced on the fence post, or leaning over to snag a drink from a running faucet, it's his cerebellum that coordinates the messages to and from his muscles to keep them all working together. And when Tiger is so excited about wrestling with a ball of yarn that he tumbles off the couch, you can chalk that up as a cerebellum fail!

BRAIN STEM:

It's warm and comfy in the sunny spot by the window, and Tiger is fast asleep. Some parts of his brain may be resting, but his brain stem is still going strong. The brain stem controls the most basic functions, like breathing, heart rate, and swallowing, so it never gets a rest.

Who says tricks are for dogs? A cat named Didga, in New South Wales, Australia, holds a world record for the number of tricks done in a minute. She can high-five, wave, roll over, sit, stay, and even ride a skateboard.

CLICKER TRICK

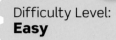

TEACH YOUR CAT A SECRET CODE

> Difficulty Level:
> **Easy**

> Active Time Needed:
> **30 minutes (spread over 4 days)**

TIP
Keep the pen you are using for this experiment in a safe place, so no one will accidentally take it to school!

Cats have a knack for knowing when dinner is on the way. Your cat may recognize the rustle of a food bag or the whir of a can opener from four rooms away. At mealtime, you may find him rubbing against your legs and meowing before you've even had a chance to pick up his bowl. You can use that enthusiasm for eating to establish a secret code between you and your cat. Then you can use that code to teach him other tricks.

YOU NEED

ballpoint pen that makes a loud "click" sound
treats

INSTRUCTIONS

1 Hold the ballpoint in one hand and a treat in the other. Click the pen and then immediately hand your cat the treat.

2 Repeat six to eight times. The next day, repeat steps one and two using the same ballpoint pen.

3 Repeat the training sessions, with six to eight clicks and treats, for two more days. By the end of the fourth session, your cat should know that a click means you are going to give him a treat.

4 Test it out. While he is not paying attention to you, click the pen. Does he look to you for a treat?

1

WHEN IT CLICKS

Click. Treat. Click. Treat. Your cat may be thinking, "Aah, this is the life!" but she probably doesn't realize she is learning. Each time you click the pen and give her a treat, she learns that the sound and the food belong together. The click becomes a secret code for "here comes a treat." When an animal learns that two events tend to go together, like a click and a treat, scientists call it **conditioning.**

Conditioning a cat to a clicking noise makes it easier to teach her tricks. It is faster and less distracting to click a pen than it is to fumble in the treat bag. The click tells her that she did the correct trick, and gives you a moment to grab a treat. Cat trainers use their secret click code to train cats to sit on command, stand on two feet, jump through hoops, roll over, and more.

CAT CLICKER

TUNA TRAP

SEE HOW FAST YOUR CAT LEARNS

> Difficulty Level:
> **Easy**

> Active Time Needed:
> **1 hour**

Your cat wants dinner, but you are comfy on the couch and not in the mood to get up. Kitty tries rubbing against your legs and purring. No luck. He tries a meow. You still don't get the hint, so he moves to a loud *yoooowwwl!* A few yowls like that and you're willing to get up, just to stop the noise. Next time, he'll know that loud yowling is the way to go. That's learning. You can test your cat's ability to learn by giving him a puzzle and seeing if he can solve it faster with practice.

YOU NEED

small clump of tuna or other smelly
   treat that your cat loves
muffin tin
a small plastic ball, such as a Wiffle
   ball
clock or timer

INSTRUCTIONS

1 Show your cat the tuna clump and place it in one of the holes in the muffin tin. Cover the hole with the Wiffle ball. The holes in the Wiffle ball will allow your cat to see and smell the tuna.

2 Time how long it takes your cat to move the ball and get the tuna.

3 Repeat the process three more times. Record how long it takes to get to the tuna each time.

4 Compare the times. If your cat was faster on his second, third, and fourth tries, it shows that he learned how to extract the tuna quickly.

TRY, TRY AGAIN

If you were given a delicious treat trapped in a muffin tin, you'd look at the setup and see that you need to pick up the ball and grab the treat. Scientists say you have insight when you can study a problem and design a solution. Your cat has a harder time. He has to discover, step-by-step, how to get that tuna. He might try pushing down on the ball with his nose, looking to you for help, or trying to bite through the ball. Eventually he'll use his nose or paw to push the ball aside. When he sees the same setup again, he has to remember. Out of all the things he did last time, which one got him a chance to chow down? By the third or fourth try, he'll know what do. Scientists call this learning by trial and error. Your cat doesn't care what you call it. He's only in this for the treats.

CAT-ITTUDE QUIZ

> Difficulty Level:
> **Easy**

> Active Time Needed:
> **10 minutes**

DISCOVER YOUR CAT'S UNIQUE MIX OF TRAITS

Have you ever taken a quiz that tells you what kind of animal you'd be, or which magical superpower you'd have, or what ice-cream flavor describes you best? Magazines and websites are full of fun and silly tests, but research into personality and behavior is also a real science. Several groups of scientists have studied behavioral traits in cats. One of the most-used rating tools is called the Feline Behavioral Assessment and Research Questionnaire (the Fe-BARQ). The complete survey is 100 questions long and covers 23 aspects of your cat's disposition. Here are three sections you can use for a snapshot of how your cat compares to others. If you'd like to give your cat the full evaluation, grab a parent and visit *febarq.org*.

YOU NEED

pencil and paper
calculator

INSTRUCTIONS

Think about how your cat has been behaving in the last few months. How has your cat responded to each of the following situations? Answer each question by selecting from the answers below. Try to answer every question, but if you haven't seen your cat in a situation, you can pick "unknown." When you are done with each section, add up your cat's total score and divide it by the number of questions you answered (leaving out any questions you marked as unknown). Then see how your cat compares to others!

Never	Seldom	Sometimes	Usually	Always	Unknown
(0 points)	(1 point)	(2 points)	(3 points)	(4 points)	(Leave blank)

SECTION 1

SOCIABILITY WITH PEOPLE

1. MY CAT IS COMFORTABLE AND RELAXED AMONG PEOPLE IN SOCIAL GATHERINGS.

2. MY CAT IS COMFORTABLE AND RELAXED BEING PETTED BY PEOPLE MY CAT DOESN'T KNOW WELL.

3. MY CAT GREETS UNFAMILIAR ADULTS VISITING MY HOME IN A FRIENDLY MANNER (SNIFFS, RUBS, PURRS, LIES ON THE FLOOR).

4. MY CAT GREETS UNFAMILIAR CHILDREN VISITING MY HOME IN A FRIENDLY MANNER (SNIFFS, RUBS, PURRS, LIES ON THE FLOOR).

5. MY CAT APPEARS COMFORTABLE (CONFIDENT, RELAXED) WHEN PLAYING WITH CHILD(REN) WHO MY CAT KNOWS WELL.

6. MY CAT APPEARS COMFORTABLE (CONFIDENT, RELAXED) WHEN PLAYING WITH CHILD(REN) WHO MY CAT DOESN'T KNOW WELL.

7. MY CAT APPEARS COMFORTABLE (CONFIDENT, RELAXED) WHEN PLAYING WITH ADULTS WHO MY CAT DOESN'T KNOW WELL.

SECTION 2

ATTENTION SEEKING

1. MY CAT NUDGES AND/OR NUZZLES ME OR OTHER MEMBERS OF THE HOUSEHOLD WHEN WE ARE SITTING OR LYING DOWN.

2. MY CAT SEEKS OUT PHYSICAL CONTACT WITH ME OR OTHER HOUSEHOLD MEMBERS WHEN I/THEY ARE SITTING OR LYING DOWN.

SECTION 3

VOCALIZATION: "TALKING" TO PEOPLE

1. MY CAT "TALKS" TO PEOPLE USING CALLS/VOCALIZATIONS (I.E., ANSWERS WHEN SPOKEN TO BY A PERSON).

2. MY CAT ASKS (VOCALIZES, WALKS TOWARD DOOR, MAKES NOISE) TO BE LET OUTSIDE, OR IN AND OUT OF ROOMS.

3. MY CAT ASKS (VOCALIZES, WALKS TOWARD ITS BOWL OR FOOD SOURCE, MAKES NOISE) FOR FOOD WHEN HUNGRY.

4. MY CAT MEOWS LOUDLY IN FRONT OF ANY CLOSED DOOR.

HOW DOES YOUR CAT COMPARE?

Compared to other cats, is yours a chatterbox? Or more the strong, silent type? Does he crave a cuddle or prefer his space? Is he friendly with all kinds of people? The Fe-BARQ has been used with more than 2,000 cats from around the world. Compare your cat's score with the average score for each of these characteristics.

SOCIABILITY Average Score = 2.08

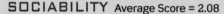

0   1   2   3   4

LONE RANGER:
It's his people or no people. Your cat doesn't want to make new friends.

SOCIAL BUTTERFLY:
Your cat loves to love and spends his time as close to humans as he can get.

ATTENTION SEEKING Average Score = 2.84

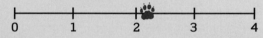

0   1   2   3   4

MR. PAWS-OFF:
Your cat may like his people fine, but he's not on a search for a snuggle.

CUDDLEBUG:
You have a "pet me, pet me, pet me" pet.

VOCALIZATION Average Score = 2.64

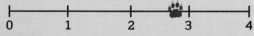

0   1   2   3   4

TIGHT-LIPPED TABBY:
You can tell him all of your secrets— his lips are sealed.

CHATTY CATTY:
Your cat has things to say and expects you to listen.

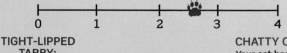

RIGHTY OR LEFTY

WHICH PAW DOES YOUR CAT PREFER?

> Difficulty Level:
> **Medium**

> Active Time Needed:
> **45 minutes**

It's not just people who favor one hand over the other. Your cat probably uses one paw more easily as well. Since you can't just hand her a pen to see how she writes, play these games to find her preferred paw.

YOU NEED

jelly jar treat trap (see p. 71)
butter or tuna treat
toy on a string
painter's tape
pencil and paper

TAKE IT FURTHER

To get strong results, scientists generally test paw preference many times over several days. One recent study tested each cat 100 times over 10 days on three different tasks. To be certain of your cat's paw preference, keep collecting data on these tasks over several days.

2

TIP
Make sure you place the jar and the toy directly in front of your cat, so she won't just use the paw closest to the object.

SAFETY NOTE
Be sure you only use painter's tape in this activity so that you don't damage her sensitive fur or skin.

INSTRUCTIONS

1 Gather your materials for all three tests. You need to repeat each experiment 10 times. For best results, switch between the activities until you have completed 10 trials of all three so your cat doesn't get bored.

2 For the first test, place the toy on a string in front of your cat. Slowly pull it away from her in a straight line. Record the first paw she uses to swipe at the toy. If she grabs with both paws at the same time, try the test again.

3 For the second test, place butter or tuna in the bottom of the jar. Set it in front of your cat. Record the first paw your cat uses to reach for the treat.

4 For the third test, place a bit of painter's tape on the bridge of your cat's nose. Record the first paw she uses to try to remove it.

5 Add the number of times your cat used her left and right paw. If she used one paw at least 20 times across all of the experiments, then your cat favors that paw.

THE RIGHT FOOT

Does your cat have a paw preference? Experiments indicate that most cats—90 percent or more—use one paw more often than the other. They seem to be divided about equally between righties and lefties, although males may be left-pawed more often than females. Cats are more likely to use their dominant hand when doing a complicated task. This is similar to a human—you might grab a book off the table with whatever hand is, well, handy. But you are going to be pickier about the hand you use with a screwdriver. Getting the treat out of the jar or wiping off her nose are complicated tasks for a cat, so she may have used the same paw for almost every try. Grabbing for a toy is less challenging, so cats are less likely to show a dominant paw for that task.

TREAT TOYS

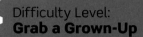

TREATS TO MAKE YOUR CAT SMARTER

Difficulty Level:
Grab a Grown-Up

Active Time Needed:
10 minutes

Your cat sure seems to have the life—lazing around all day, napping in the sun, and getting fed whenever she's hungry. But believe it or not, cats can actually get bored, just like humans. Pet stores are full of feeding toys that will keep cats moving and thinking as they eat. These feeder toys can help reduce boredom, can improve behavior in bored cats, and are a great way to get overweight cats moving. You don't have to dip into your savings for your cat to get these benefits. Build your own feeding toys using the plans below or invent your own puzzle to give Kitty a mental workout. You can put more than food in these toys; pick one to use for "Crazy for Catnip" on p. 72.

BOTTLE BOPPER

YOU NEED

plastic soda bottle
permanent marker
box cutter

INSTRUCTIONS

1 Hold a treat that you would like to use with your bottle bopper against the bottle. Use the marker to draw a square around the treat that is big enough for the treat to fit through. Draw five to seven of these squares in different places on your bottle.

2 Ask an adult to use the box cutter to cut out the squares. Make sure each hole is big enough to allow the treat to fall through.

3 Load treats into the bottle bopper through the mouth and lay it on the floor.

TIP
A hole that is much larger than the treat is good when your cat is just learning to use a feeding toy. Make one with smaller holes when she is ready for a challenge.

TOILET TISSUE TUMBLER

YOU NEED

empty toilet paper tube
safety scissors
masking tape

> Difficulty Level:
> **Easy**

> Active Time Needed:
> **5 minutes**

INSTRUCTIONS

1 Draw four one-inch (2.5-cm) lines at equal distances around one end of the toilet paper tube. Cut along each line to make four small flaps.

2 Fold the flaps so that each flap overlaps the one before it. Tuck the last flap all the way under the first flap.

3 Press the flaps tightly to make a flat bottom and secure them with tape.

4 Place treats or catnip into the tube and set it upright. Fluffy will have to knock the tube over and roll it around to get to the goodies.

JELLY JAR TREAT TRAP

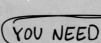

YOU NEED

jar or heavy cup

> Difficulty Level:
> **Easy**

> Active Time Needed:
> **5 minutes**

INSTRUCTIONS

1 Find a jar or cup with an opening that is too small for your cat to stick his head in, but large enough for his paw. It should also be no more than about five inches (12 cm) tall and be heavy enough that it will not fall over easily. Jelly jars often fit these size requirements.

2 Place some form of wet food, such as tuna, canned cat food, or butter, into the bottom of the jar.

3 Watch as your cat dips his paw in to retrieve the treat!

CRAZY FOR CATNIP

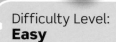

FIND OUT WHETHER YOUR CAT HAS THE CATNIP GENE

> **Difficulty Level:**
> **Easy**

> **Active Time Needed:**
> **20 minutes**

The internet is crawling with videos of cats sniffing, rolling, kicking, and drooling over catnip. But in reality, only about 70 to 80 percent of cats respond to it. The response is genetic—if one cat in the family isn't interested in catnip, the rest are also likely to give it a pass. Where does your cat stand on the catnip issue? Make some feeder toys and find out.

YOU NEED

fresh or dried catnip
two identical feeder toys (make them using the instructions on pp. 70–71)

INSTRUCTIONS

1 Place one tablespoon of fresh or dried catnip into one of the feeder toys. Leave the second toy empty.

2 Place the two toys on the floor about two feet (0.6 m) apart.

3 Bring in your cat and observe how much time he spends with each toy in a two-minute period.

4 Observe how much of the time he spends interacting with each toy.

CATNIP ON MY MIND

What is it about catnip that gives cats the crazies? It all starts with a substance in the leaves called nepetalactone. Cats inhale it into their nose and vomeronasal organ. It triggers the scent detectors and sends a message to the brain. Scientists aren't sure what that message is, but they suspect the nepetalactone is similar to some pheromones—specifically the chemicals cats use to signal to each other when they are ready to mate. So all that rolling and sniffing may be your cat thinking he has found true love.

Catnip plants aren't trying to give your cat a love potion. Nepetalactone is an insect repellent. The plant releases the chemical to try to stop insects that might want to munch on its leaves. It works, too. Researchers have found that nepetalactone can be used as a mosquito repellent and roach spray.

TAKE IT FURTHER
If your cat is a catnip fan, try stocking the feeder with catnip and hiding it. How long does it take for your cat to find it?

3

OTHER PLEASING PLANTS

Most cats who fall for catnip fall hard. If your cat doesn't spend most of that minute with the catnip toy, you've got a nonresponder. The good news: There are other plants that you can use to give Kitty a treat. Silver vine, which is related to kiwifruit, may be even more powerful than catnip. In one study, more cats responded to silver vine *and* they had a more extreme response. Other cats have catnip-like reactions to valerian root and Tatarian honeysuckle. Ninety-four percent of cats react to at least one of the four plants.

SILVER VINE

in the LAB

PLAY WITH ME!

The way to a dog's heart is through his stomach. If you give a dog a treat, he'll be your friend for life. But what is the deep desire of a cat? Kristyn Vitale, a researcher at Oregon State University, decided to find out, and she began with her own Maine-coon mix named Macy.

Vitale identified four categories that cats might enjoy: interesting smells, toys, food, and human interaction. She picked several examples of each for Macy to choose between. For example, in the smell category, Macy was brought into a room with three cloths. One smelled like a gerbil. One had the scent of another cat. And one bore the inviting odor of catnip. For three minutes, Macy explored the cloths. Macy dismissed the gerbil and the other cat with a sniff and headed for the catnip.

Vitale repeated the procedure with three toys (a mouse, a loose feather, and a moving feather) and three food items (chicken, tuna, and a store-bought soft treat). She also tested three ways a pet owner could interact with her cat: petting, playing together with a feather, and listening to encouraging words. This category was tested a little differently, so that the same human could offer each interaction. She offered each interaction for one minute and timed how long Macy chose to participate.

THE SWEET SMELL OF CATNIP

In the food matchup, tuna won! Over half of the cats in Vitale's research picked tuna over store-bought treats.

Cats who do not have owners, called **feral cats**, are more selective about food than pet cats. When they have a chance, they will eat a little bit of a variety of foods rather than gorging on one kind. This helps them get a balanced diet.

HEAD-TO-HEAD MATCHUP

Once Vitale had Macy's preferences in all four categories, she was ready to put those items up against each other in a head-to-head match. She divided the floor into four sections and placed one of Macy's favorites into each. Macy had three more minutes to spend as she desired. And what she desired, out of all of her favorites, was being petted by Vitale.

Vitale repeated this procedure with 50 cats: 25 pets and 25 from a shelter. Each cat picked a favorite from each category and then picked from among the favorites. Half the cats preferred human interaction over all other options, even food!

CATS REALLY LOVE THEIR PEOPLE TIME.

TASTY TUNA

POWERFUL PREFERENCES

This is good news for cat owners and cat friends. Cats really like us! It's also good news for cat researchers. There has been less research into how cats think and learn than there has been for other animals, such as dogs. Cat researchers often borrow techniques used with other animals. They don't always work. "With dogs, it's just food and more food," said Vitale. "We realized, maybe this is not the best for cats."

With these findings, Vitale hopes that researchers can do a better job of encouraging cats to participate in studies that might bring cat lovers more good news about their frisky felines.

ADAPTATION: a trait that helps an animal be successful in its environment

CONDITIONING: learning to associate an action or event with a reward or punishment

CREPUSCULAR: awake and active at dawn and dusk

DIAPHRAGM: muscle that contracts to make the chest cavity bigger and expand the lungs

FERAL CATS: domestic cats who live around humans without an owner

FLEHMEN RESPONSE: the process cats use to breathe air into their vomeronasal organ

GLAND: an organ that releases a chemical, such as oil

HEMISPHERES: the left and right sides of the brain

OBJECT PERMANENCE: understanding that an object exists even when it disappears from view

OLFACTORY MEMBRANE: the part of the nose that has odor sensors

PAPILLAE: bumps on the tongue (one such bump is called a papilla)

PHEROMONES: chemicals that animals use to communicate with each other through smell

PINNAE: the exterior part of a cat's ear

PROSTHETIC: an artificial body part, like a titanium leg

PUPIL: the part of the eye that lets in light

REFLEX: an animal's automatic response

RESPIRATION: breathing

RETINA: the part of the eye that captures information from light

TAPETUM: a reflective layer in a cat's eye that helps it capture more light in dim settings

TERRITORY: a portion of land that an animal reserves for itself for hunting, mating, or nesting, and will defend against other animals of the same species

VERTEBRAE: the bones that make up the spine

VESTIBULAR ORGAN: the sense organ for balance

VIBRISSAE: long, stiff hairs that provide a cat information via touch

VOMERONASAL ORGAN: a smelling organ devoted to smelling pheromones

WEAN: getting an animal used to food other than its mother's milk

WHISKING: the process of moving vibrissae around to sense the environment

DISCOVER MORE ABOUT CATS

Books

Carney, Elizabeth. *Everything Big Cats.* National Geographic Kids, 2011.

Newman, Aline Alexander. *Cat Tales: True Stories of Kindness and Companionship With Kitties.* National Geographic Kids, 2017.

Newman, Aline Alexander, and Gary Weitzman. *How to Speak Cat: A Guide to Decoding Cat Language.* National Geographic Kids, 2015.

MORE SCIENCE EXPERIMENTS FROM NATIONAL GEOGRAPHIC

Wheeler-Toppen, Jodi. *Dog Science Unleashed: Fun Activities to Do With Your Canine Companion.* National Geographic Kids, 2018.

Young, Karen Romano. *Try This! 50 Fun Experiments for the Mad Scientist in You.* National Geographic Kids, 2014.

——. *Try This! Extreme: 50 Fun and Safe Experiments for the Mad Scientist in You.* National Geographic Kids, 2017.

ONLINE

CatTracker
CatTracker.org
You can check out current cat science studies, and even register to participate in one with your favorite feline at the home of this cat science research group.

FeBarq
FeBarq.com
Learn more about the Feline Behavioral Assessment and Research Questionnaire and give your cat the entire test.

National Geographic Kids
natgeokids.com/pets
Visit the Pet Central portal to play games, take quizzes, read awesome articles, and learn fantastic facts about pets of all shapes and sizes!

The Truth About Cats
channel.nationalgeographic.com/wild/the-truth-about-cats
Read, see clips, and learn from this National Geographic miniseries on cats.

INDEX